101 HILARIOUS ANIMAL JOKES & RIDDLES FOR KIDS

Laugh Out Loud With These Funny & Silly Jokes: Even Your Pet Will Laugh! (WITH 35+ PICTURES)

Johnny Riddle

© **Copyright 2020** by Johnny Riddle – All rights reserved.

In no way is it legal to reproduce, duplicate, or transmit any part of this document in either electronic means or in printed format. Recording of this publication is strictly prohibited and any storage of this document is not allowed unless with written permission from the publisher.

The information provided herein is stated to be truthful and consistent, in that any liability, in terms of inattention or otherwise, by any usage or abuse of any policies, processes, or directions contained within is the solitary and utter responsibility of the recipient reader. Under no circumstances will any legal responsibility or blame be held against the author for any reparation, damages, or monetary loss due to the information herein, either directly or indirectly.

The information herein is offered for informational purposes solely, and is universal as so. The presentation of the information is without contract or any type of guarantee assurance.

Legal Disclaimer: images by Freepik or licensed for commercial use.

Table of Contents

INTRODUCTION	4
101 HILARIOUS ANIMAL JOKES & RIDDLES	7
BONUS JOKES	120
DID YOU LIKE THIS BOOK?	135
OTHER JOKE BOOKS BY JOHNNY RIDDLE	137

INTRODUCTION

First joke: *What dog loves to take bubble baths?*

Answer: A shampoodle!

Thank you for picking up a copy of '*101 Clean Hilarious Animal Jokes & Riddles For Kids*'.

Are you ready to have a good laugh with these funny animal jokes?

All <u>kids love animals</u>. Also, all kids <u>love to laugh</u>.

Plus...<u>Laughter is good</u> for you!

You probably already knew that. I mean, who doesn't feel good when they laugh, right?

But did you know that laughter is associated with all these health benefits?

Laughter:

- relaxes your body
- boosts your immune system
- triggers the release of feel-good hormones, such as endorphins
- protects your heart

When you're reading these jokes with your kids, you're *also* working on their health!

Sounds good, right?

If you're looking for a good laugh about animals, you've come to the right place!

This book is jam-packed with:

- 100+ hilarious animal jokes, and
- 35+ funny illustrations

that all kids will love.

So, I hope you and your kids are ready to *roar with laughter.* **let's get started with the first animal joke!**

101 HILARIOUS ANIMAL JOKES & RIDDLES

1.

A first-grade teacher was telling her students the story of the 2005 animated movie 'Chicken Little.' She got to the part when Chicken Little ran up to the farmer, saying: "The sky is falling. The sky is falling."

Then the teacher paused, looked around the class, and asked the kids what they thought the farmer said in reply.

One little boy raised his hand and said: "I think the farmer said: Holy cow, a talking chicken!"

2.

A duck went to the post office to send a telegram. He took out a blank form and wrote: "Quack. Quack. Quack. Quack. Quack. Quack. Quack. Quack. Quack."

When the duck was done, he gave it to the clerk. The clerk looked at the paper and said to the duck: "Listen, there are only 9 words here. We have a special offer today. You could send another 'Quack' for the same price."

3.

Q: What did the waiter say to the dog when he brought out her food?

A: Bone appétit!

4.

Two peacocks are sitting on opposite sides of a river. One peacock yells to the other: "How do I get to the other side of the river?" The other peacock replies: "You ARE on the other side!"

5.

A King, who's is very fond of all kinds of animals and has its own zoo, hosts a Royal Dinner Party for all the important people in the country.

To impress his guests, he has asked his staff to put some of his most-loved animals in the party room.

One of the animals in the room, an Orangutan, lets out a loud fart.

The King turns to him and says: "How dare you fart in front of me!"

The Orangutan replies: "I'm terribly sorry, your Highness, I didn't realize it was your turn!"

6.

Knock, Knock.

Who's there?

Giraffe.

Giraffe who?

Giraffe something to eat? I'm super hungry!

7.

Did you hear about the owl who invented the Knock-Knock joke?

He won the no-bell prize!

8.

Q: What do you call a dog with a surround system?

A: A sub-woofer!

9.

Two friends were walking their dogs on a Friday afternoon. One had a Bulldog and the other had a Chihuahua.

Then the guy with the Bulldog said: "I'm thirsty, let's get a drink in that bar over there." To which his friend replied: "I don't think they will allow our dogs in there." The one with the Bulldog responded: "Just follow my lead, trust me."

The guy with the Bulldog put on a pair of sunglasses and walked into the bar.

The bouncer at the door said: "I'm sorry man, but there are no pets allowed inside." The man with the Bulldog replied: "But this is my guide dog, I am helpless without him!". Bouncer: "A Bulldog?"

The man replied: "Yeah, they're using Bulldogs now too, they're amazing!". Bouncer: "Okay, come on in."

The other man then also put on his sunglasses. He thought: a Chihuahua is even more unlikely to be a guide dog, but it's worth a try. So the bouncer stopped him, and said: "Sorry no pets allowed." To which the man replied: "This is my guide dog, I am lost without him." Bouncer: "Really, a Chihuahua?". To which the man replied: "Whhaaat? They gave me a fricking Chihuahua?!"

10.

Q: What do you get when you cross a chicken with a Martian?

A: An eggs-traterrestrial!

11.

Q: Where do lizards go when their tails fall off?

A: The re-tail store.

12.

A python snake sits in a bar, sipping a Mojito cocktail.

A customer walks up to the snake and says, "Wow, it's not often that I see a snake drinking a cocktail here!"

To which the snake replies: "Yeah, but that's hardly a surprise at these prices."

13.

Q: What is every cat's favorite movie?

A: The Purrrr-minator!

14.

Q: How does a lion greet the other animals in the field?

A: "Pleased to eat you!"

15.

While mending fences out on the range, a very religious cowboy lost his favorite Bible. He was devastated!

A week later, however, a monkey walked up to him, carrying that same Bible in its mouth.

The cowboy was astonished, he couldn't believe it! He took the precious book out of the monkey's mouth, thanked him, went on his knees and exclaimed: "It's a miracle!".

To which the monkey replied: "Not really. Your name is written inside the cover."

16.

Q: What do you call a dog who designs buildings?

A: A bark-itect!

17.

The teacher asks the class to make a drawing of a cow in the grass.

After about 30 minutes, the teacher walks around to see the results. He pauses when he sees Johnny's drawing: "The assignment was to draw a cow and grass, Johnny, but I only see a cow on your drawing. Where is grass?"

Johnny: "The cow ate all the grass, teacher."

18.

Q: Why do French people love to eat snails?

A: Because they don't like fast food!

19.

One day, a man was driving on a country road when he looked out of the window and noticed a chicken running alongside his car. He was amazed to see the chicken keeping up with him: he was driving 40 mph! So, he accelerated to 50. But the chicken stayed right next to him. Even more astonished, he now sped up to 60 mph, but the chicken not only kept up with, it even passed him!

Then the man noticed something peculiar: the chicken had 3 legs. He decided to follow the chicken and finally ended up at a farm. When he got out of his car and looked around, he was even more shocked: all the chickens on this farm had three legs!

He approached the farmer and asked: "Why do all these chickens have 3 legs?"

The farmer replied: "Well, I figured: everybody likes chicken legs, right? So, I decided to breed a three-legged bird. I'm going to be a rich!"

Then the man asked him how the chicken legs tasted. Then farmer said, with a sad expression on his face: "I don't know, I haven't caught one yet..."

20.

Today was a special day: it was a young mosquito's first day to leave the home and fly out.

He stayed away all day. When he finally came home, his mother asked him, "You've been away so long, how was your journey?"

The young mosquito replied, "It was amazing, mom. Everyone was clapping for me!"

21.

Q: What do you call a cat that lives in an igloo?

A: An eskimeow!

22.

Q: What do you call a dog magician?

A: A labracadabrador!

23.

A policeman in Los Angeles stops a man in a Mustang with a lion in the front seat.

"What are you doing with that lion?" he asked, "You should take it to the zoo."

The following week, the same policeman sees the same man with the lion again in the front seat. This time, both of them are wearing sunglasses.

The policeman pulls him over again, upset: "I thought you were going to take that lion to the zoo!" The man replied: "I did. We had such a good time we are going to the beach this weekend!"

24.

One day, a panda walks into a dinner, takes a seat, and orders roasted chicken. He eats the chicken, then pulls out his gun, and shoots the waiter dead.

As the panda stands up to leave, the manager yells, "Hey panda! Where on earth do you think you are going? You just shot my waiter and you also didn't pay for the chicken!"

The panda responded, "Relax, will you? I'm a panda. Look it up!"

The manager opens a dictionary and searches for panda. It reads, "A tree climbing mammal that lives in Asia, with black and white colors. Eats, shoots, and leaves."

25.

Q: If a Transformer lived in the deep sea, what would you call it?

A: Octopus Prime!

26.

Q: Why do geese fly to the south when winter comes?

A: Because it is too far to walk there.

27.

Psychiatrist: What seems to be the problem?

Patient: I think I'm a chicken.

Psychiatrist: How long has this been going on?

Patient: Ever since I came out of my shell.

28.

Two moms discuss how to get their sons to wake up in the morning, to get them to school on time.

"How do you get your sleepy-head son up in the morning?", the first mom asked. The other mom replied: "I just put the cat on the bed."

"Huh, how does that help?"

The other mom: "The dog's already there..."

29.

An 83-year old man is walking through a forest when he spots a frog. Not just any frog, this frog can talk! As he picks up the frog, it says, "Nice to meet you, mister. If you kiss me, I will turn into a beautiful photo model and be yours for a week."

Instead of kissing the frog, the old man puts the frog in the pocket of his jacket. The frog screams, "Hey, I have a better deal: if you kiss me now, I will turn into a super-hot photo model and kiss you every day for a whole month!"

The old man takes the frog out of his pocket, looks it in the left eye, and says, "At my old age, I prefer having a talking frog!"

30.

Q: What do you get if you milk a pampered cow?

A: Spoiled milk!

31.

Q: What did the alien say to the cat?

A: "Take me to your litter."

32.

Q: Why does a hummingbird hum?

A: Because he doesn't know any of the words!

33.

Q: What's a dog's favorite kind of pizza?

A: Pupperoni!

34.

A pig farmer is showing a prospective buyer around, when the buyer spots a pig in the yard with a wooden leg. The buyer asks, "Why does that pig have a wooden leg?"

The farmer responds, "Now this pig is something special. It is so smart, I let it drive my tractor to work the land."

"Great," the buyer says, "But why does it have a wooden leg?"

The farmer replies: "This pig is so smart, it has a degree in law *and* biology."

"Truly amazing!", the buyer responds, "But tell me, what's up with the wooden leg?"

"Well," the farmer says, "When you have a pig that is that smart, you don't eat it all at once!"

35.

Q: What did the mother cow say to the baby cow in the cowshed?

A: "Time to close your eyes, it is pasture bedtime."

36.

Q: Why do centipedes have 200 legs?

A: In order to walk.

37.

Q: What is the fastest dog in the world?

A: A Labraghini.

38.

Q: What do you call a dog with a surround system?

A: A sub-woofer.

39.

Q: What is a cat's favorite car?

A: Catillac!

40.

Q: What do you call a bull that is sound asleep?

A: Bulldozer!

41.

Returning from the market, the farmer's son was dropped the crate of chickens his father had entrusted to him. The box broke open, and the chickens scurried off in different directions.

The boy panicked for a few seconds, but then quickly got back to his senses. Determined not to disappoint his father, he walked all over the neighborhood scooping up the wayward birds and returning them to the repaired crate.

Finally, the boy – reluctantly – returned home. He hoped he had found them all, but expected the worst.

He felt it was best to just speak up: "Pa, the chickens got loose," the boy confessed sadly, "but I managed to find all twelve of them."

"Well, you did really well son," the farmer replied. "You left with only seven this morning!"

42.

Q: What do an elephant and a tree have in common?

A: Both have trunks!

43.

A man takes his Saint Bernard Dog to the vet, because he is cross-eyed.

The vet says: "Let's have a look" and picks up the Saint Bernard to examine his eyes. After looking at his eyes for a while, the vet says: "I'm going to have to put him down."

"Wait, what?" the man replies, "Just because he is cross-eyed?"

Vet: "No, because he is really heavy!"

44.

Q: How do little bees travel to school?

A: They take the school buzz!

45.

Q: What do you call a pig that goes to the gym to practice karate every week?

A: A pork chop.

46.

A man is visiting the zoo, when, all of a sudden, he sees people running around in panic, in all directions. Quickly, he learns why: a tiger is on the loose! And it looks hungry...

The man starts running, too. Unfortunately, the tiger starts chasing him. The man runs as fast as he can, and decides to say a little prayer, "Please, if you can, turn this tiger into a Christian, Father."

He turns over his shoulder, and a miracle has happened: the tiger is on its knees! Happy to see his prayer answered, the man stops running and walks towards the tiger. As he comes closer, he overhears the tiger saying a prayer: "Thank you, Father, for the food I am about to receive."

47.

Q: What's a cat's favorite dessert?

A: Mice Cream!

48.

Q: Why do rabbits make terrible dance partners?

A: They've got two left feet!

49.

Two cats are sitting in front of bird's cage and observe a newly arrived green canary. One cat says to the other, "It really is a strange color for a bird. Maybe he's not ripe yet."

50.

Q: What type of key can open a banana?

A: A monkey!

51.

On a dark night, a burglar breaks into a house.

As he reaches to steal some valuables, he hears a voice say: "Jesus is watching you."

Alarmed by the voice, the burglar jumps up and hides behind the curtain. He peaks around the corner but doesn't see anybody.

So, he goes back to the valuables and continues putting them in his bag.

"Jesus is watching you," the voice says once more.

This time, the burglar looks harder and he sees a parrot.

"Who are you?" he asks.

The parrot replies, "Elijah."

"Wait, what? Who on earth would call a parrot Elijah?" the burglar responds, relieved that he is only chatting with a parrot.

"I don't know," says Elijah, "I guess the same kind of people that would call a Rottweiler Jesus."

52.

Two bats are hanging upside down in a dark cave. After some small talk, they start reflecting on their lives.

One bat asks the other, "Do you remember the worst thing that happened to you last year?"

The other bat replies, "Yes, it was the day I had diarrhea!"

53.

Q: What do you think difference is between an acoustic guitar and a fish?

A: You can tune a guitar, but you cannot tuna fish!

54.

A traveler sits down in a restaurant to get lunch. All of a sudden, a bear walks in, buys a vanilla ice cream and leaves.

The traveler is astounded: "Wow, that's so strange!"

The restaurant manager: "Yeah, I agree, up until today he always ordered banana ice cream."

55.

One day, a police officer was sitting in his car with his K9 partner in the back seat. A little girl approached the car and asked the officer: "Is that a dog in the back seat?"

The officer replied: "Yep, it sure is!"

To which the girl responded: "Wow, what did he do?"

56.

Q: What did the cat on the smart phone say?

A: "Can you hear meow?"

57.

Q: What do you call an alligator wearing a black vest?

A: An investigator!

58.

Q: If a monkey explodes, what do you call it?

A: Baboom!

59.

An elementary school teacher wants to educate her class about animals.

School teacher: "Children, what does a chicken give us?"

Bill: "Eggs!"

School teacher: "Very good, Bill! Class, what does a pig give you?"

Susan: "Bacon!"

School teacher: "Well done, Susan! Anyone else: what does the cow give you?"

George: "Homework!"

School teacher: "…"

60.

Gareth: "Jane, why do you think rhinos wear pink polish?"

Jane: "I don't have a clue."

Gareth: "To hide in cherry trees."

Jane: "Come on, Gareth. I have never seen a rhino sitting in a cherry tree."

Gareth: "See, it works!"

61.

One day, a flamingo walks in a supermarket and asks the shop assistant if he sells cranberries. The shop assistant says, "No, we do have raspberries and strawberries, but we don't sell cranberries." The flamingo goes home and returns the next day, "Good day, do you sell cranberries?". Again, the shop assistant says they don't.

The flamingo leaves the shop, and returns the very next day. "Oh no, there he is again," says the shop assistant to himself. And sure enough, the flamingo asks the shop assistant if the supermarket sells cranberries.

This time, though, the shop assistant is so fed up with this annoying flamingo that he says, "No, flamingo, we don't sell cranberries! And if you come back tomorrow and ask me this same question again, I swear I will nail your beak to the floor of the supermarket!"

The flamingo goes home again. The shop assistant can't believe his eyes when he sees the flamingo walk through the door again, the next day. This time, the flamingo asks, "Do you have any nails?" The shop assistant says, "No, we don't have any nails."

"Okay, good," the flamingo says, "Do you sell cranberries?"

62.

Q: What do you call a group of chickens clucking in unison?

A: A Hensemble!

63.

Q: How are a dog and a marine biologist alike?

A: One wags a tail and the other tags a whale.

64.

Q: What is the favorite meal of a whale?

A: A peanut butter and jellyfish sandwich!

65.

Q: Why are cats so good at video games?

A: Because they have nine lives!

66.

A polar bear walks into a job center. "Wow, a talking polar bear," says the clerk. "With your talent, we will definitely be able to find you a job in the circus."

"The circus?" says the polar bear, disappointed: "Why would a circus want to hire an electrician?"

67.

A man sits down in a movie theater when he sees a penguin walk in, who sits down in the seat next to him. "Are you really a penguin?" the man asks, surprised. "I am", said the penguin.

"What are you doing at this movie?", the man then asked.

The penguin replied, "Well, I liked the book."

68.

School teacher: "Class, who can name a bird with wings that cannot fly?"

Donald: "I can, sir. A dead bird!"

69.

One day, a man visited his friend. When he walked into the living room, he found his friend playing checkers with a camel.

Astonished, he watched the game for a couple of minutes. "I can't believe my eyes!" he exclaimed. "That is the smartest camel I have ever seen."

To which his friend replied: "Mwoah, he's not that smart. I've beaten him three games out of five."

70.

One day, a construction worker and a puma walk into a bar. The construction worker orders two whiskeys, one for him and one for the puma.

After they've finished a few more drinks, the puma falls down on the ground. The construction worker grabs his jacked, puts some money on the bar, and heads for the door.

"Hey," the bartender yells, "Hold it right there! You can't leave that lying on the floor."

"Dude," the man replies, as he walks out of the door, "that's not a lion, it's a puma."

71.

Have you heard about the clam that excelled at playing piano?

It has great mussel memory!

72.

Q: What did the cat say when he lost his toys?

A: You got to be kitten me.

73.

Q: One day, a rooster crossed the border from Canada to the USA to lay an egg. To which country does the egg belong?

A: None. Roosters don't lay eggs!

74.

One day, a baby snake moves closer to his mom, and asks "Mama, is our bite poisonous?" The mama snake replied, "Yes baby, but why do you ask me that?"

The baby snake responded, "Ehm, because I just bit myself in the tail, mommy…"

75.

Q: How do we know that eating carrots is good for your eyes?

A: Because no one has ever seen a rabbit wear glasses!

76.

Q: What do you call a scary chicken?

A: A poultrygeist.

77.

Q: Why was the animal removed from the card game in the casino?

A: Because he was a cheetah!

78.

A boy fly takes a girl fly out on a date. As they are flying through town, they spot fresh dog poop on the sidewalk. Quickly, They rush down and start feasting.

All of a sudden, the boy fly stops eating, and a squeamish smile appears on his face. The girl fly asks, "What's up, are you feeling all right?"

Then, the girl fly notices a funky smell and says, "I can't believe it. We're on a date and you fart during dinner!"

79.

One evening, a man hears the doorbell ring. He walks to the door and opens it. As he looks down, he sees a snail. He picks it up and throws it away, as far as he can.

Two years later, the doorbell rings again. The man opens the door, looks down, and there's that same snail again. The snail says, "Hey, that was so rude. What did you do that for?"

80.

Q: What do you get when you cross a dog and a calculator?

A: A friend you can count on!

81.

A man drives deep into the woods to get rid of his cat. He lets her out at an abandoned place. After 30 minutes, his wife calls him: "The cat is back..."

The man growls: "Oh man...Ehm, can you put her on please? I got lost and need directions."

82.

Q: What would you get if you crossed a giraffe with an ant?

A: A giant!

83.

Q: What did the queen bee say to the lazy working bee?

A: Beehive yourself!

84.

Q: Where are chicks born?

A: In Chick-cago.

85.

Two criminals are about to break out of prison. The first one jumps off a wall into a trash container. The guard, alarmed by the noise, shouts "Who's there?". The criminal replies, "Woof Woof!" The guard is relieved, "Ah I see, it's just a dog."

Then, the second criminal jumps, also making some noise. The guard now gets suspicious and asks, "Hello, who is there?" To which the second criminal replies, "Nobody, it's just the dog again!"

86.

Q: What do you get when you cross a cow with a shark?

A: Nobody knows, but it's best not to try and milk it!

87.

Q: Where do a bull and cow take their calves when they go on a holiday?

A: The aMOOsement park!

88.

A couple were going to see a movie and ordered a taxi. As the couple left the house, their cat ran back in. The husband went back inside, because they didn't want the cat to be shut in the house while they were away. The wife stepped into the taxi.

Because she didn't want the taxi driver to know that the house was empty, she told him that her husband had just gone inside to say goodbye to her mother.

A short while later, her husband also stepped into the cab and said: "My apologies for taking so long, but that stupid old thing was hiding under the bed. I had to poke her with a broomstick to get her to come out!"

89.

Q: One day, a skunk walked into the courtroom. How did the judge respond?

A: He said: "Odor in the court!"

90.

Two goldfish are in a tank. One goldfish ask the other goldfish, "Can you help me out here? I have never driven this thing!"

91.

A man runs into the office of a psychiatrist and says: "Doctor, you have to help me: My wife thinks she's a chicken and I don't know what to do!"

The psychiatrist, still somewhat shocked from the man bursting into his room: "Ehm, I see. How long has she had this condition?"

"Two years," says the man.

"Two years, you say?! Then why did it take you so long to come and see me?" asked the psychiatrist.

The man shrugs his shoulders and replies: "We needed the eggs."

92.

Q: What do you call a cat that gets anything it wants?

A: Purrr-suasive!

93.

Q: What do you call a large dog that meditates?

A: Aware wolf.

94.

One day, a man comes home with a talking parrot he just bought in a pet shop.

He is really excited about his new pet, and immediately starts trying to teach him some cool things to say.

However, he quickly finds out the parrot has a bad mouth: all the parrot does is swear at him!

After a few days of trying, the man gets fed up and says, "Listen, parrot, if you continue to swear at me, I have no other choice but to punish you by putting you in the freezer."

The parrot, unimpressed, continues his bad behavior. So, finally, the man follows through on his threat and puts the bird in the freezer.

After an hour has passed, the parrot knocks on the door and asks if the man can open it. When the man does, the shivering parrot says, "I am sorry, sorry, SORRY! I will never curse again. Can you tell me what that chicken did?!"

95.

A duck was sentenced to a 5-year jail sentence.

At lunch, one of the other inmates starts talking with him and asks, "So, what you are in for?"

The duck replied, "I got caught selling quack."

96.

Q: What's the name for a rabbit with fleas?

A: Bugs Bunny!

97.

Q: Everyone knows oysters never donate anything to charities. Do you know why?

A: They are shellfish!

98.

Q: What are a frog's favorite type of sandals?

A: Open-toad sandals!

99.

3 crickets were sitting together on a tree branch.

The first cricket, "Chirp." Next, the second cricket said, "Chirp." Then, the third cricket said, "Chirp, chirp."

The first cricket said, "Hey, smarty pants, don't change the subject!"

100.

Q: What do you get when you cross a cat with a parrot?

A: A carrot.

101.

A policeman stops a man in a car with an elephant in the front seat. "Sir, can you please explain what are you doing with that elephant?", he asked. "You should take it to the zoo!"

The next week, the police officer sees the same man again, with the elephant in the front seat. This time, both are wearing sunglasses.

The policeman pulls the car over. "I thought you were going to take it to the zoo!" The man replied, "I did. We had such a great time we are going to the beach this weekend!"

BONUS JOKES

These are <u>11 bonus jokes</u> from my popular book *'101 Hilarious Clean Jokes & Riddles for Kids.'*

Enjoy!

***

1.

A teacher asks her class: "Let's say I gave you two dogs, two more dogs, and then another two dogs; how many would you have?"

Wilma answers: "Seven."

Teacher: "No, Wilma, let me repeat the question... If I gave you 2 dogs, 2 more dogs and then another 2, how many would you have in total?"

Wilma: "7."

Teacher, getting frustrated now: "Pff, OK...Let's try this another way. If I gave you two bananas, two more bananas, and then another two, how many bananas would you have?"

Wilma: "Six."

Teacher: "Exactly! Now, if I gave you two dogs, two more, and another two; how many would you have?"

Wilma: "Seven!"

Teacher: "Wilma, where on earth do you get seven from?!"

Wilma: "Because I already have a dog at home!"

2.

Q: Why wasn't the blonde able to add 5 + 10 on her calculator?

A: Because she couldn't figure out where the "10" button was!

3.

Q: What does a computer eat when it's hungry?

A: Microchips!

4.

Did you read the newspaper, about the woman whose whole left-side was cut off?

She's all right now….

5.

A young boy came home from school, with a black eye. "What happened?", his mother asked

"I had a big fight with my classmate," the boy replied, "He called me a sissy."

"And, what did you do?", the mother asked.

The little boy said, "I hit him with my purse!"

6.

Q: Why did all the students in class kids eat their homework?

A: Because their teacher told them: "It's a piece of cake!"

7.

Joshua: "Did you the news item about the kidnapping at school?"

Shane: "Yes, I saw it. You don't need to worry about it though. He just woke up."

8.

Mr. and Mrs. Huddlefield had a happy marriage, with two sons. Don't ask why, but when they were born they gave them very unique names: they named their first son 'Trouble', and the other son 'Mind Your Own Business'.

The boys were best friends. One day, they decided to play 'Hide and Seek'. 'Trouble' hid while 'Mind Your Own Business' counted to sixty. After he finished counting, 'Mind Your Own Business' began looking for his brother. He started with bushes, small corners, and even garbage cans. When he couldn't find him, he started looking in and under cars.

This was when he caught the attention of a police officer on duty.

The officer approached him, and asked: "Hey there, what are you doing?" "Playing a game," the boy replied.

"What is your name?" the officer then asked. "Mind Your Own Business." Furious, and with a raised voice, the police offer then asked, "Are you looking for trouble?!"

To which the boy replied, "Yes, I am!"

9.

One day, a little girl is sitting at the kitchen table when she asks her father, "How were people born?"

Her father replied, "Well, Adam and Eve made babies, then their babies became adults and made babies, and that's how people were born."

That afternoon, the girl was having tea with her mother and asked her the same question. Her mom answered, "At first, we were monkeys, but then we evolved to become like we are now."

When her father got home from work, the little girl ran to him and yelled, "Dad, you lied to me!"

After she had explained what happened, her father replied, "I didn't lie to you. Your mom was only talking about her side of the family."

10.

One day, a woman walked into a lawyer's office and said, "My colleague owes me $400 and she won't pay up. I'm here for legal advice; what should I do?"

The lawyer thought about it for a few seconds, and then asked: "Do you have any proof you loaned her the money?". "Unfortunately, I don't," the woman replied.

"OK, then here's what you should do. Write her an email asking her for the $4,000 she owes you," the lawyer said.

"Huh, she only owes me $400, though" the woman replied.

"Indeed. That's what she will reply. And that email will be your proof!"

11.

Q: A boy volcano was located next to a girl volcano. What did he say to her?

A: "I lava you..."

***

This is the end of this bonus chapter.

Want to continue reading?

Then get your copy of "101 Hilarious Clean Jokes & Riddles for Kids" at your favorite bookstore!

DID YOU LIKE THIS BOOK?

If you enjoyed this book, I would like to ask you for a favor. Please leave a review online!

Reviews are the lifeblood of independent authors. *I know*, you're short on time. But I would <u>really appreciate</u> even just a few sentences!

Your voice is important for this book to reach as many people as possible.

The more reviews this book gets, the more people will be able to find it and have a good laugh with these funny jokes!

***

IF YOU DID NOT LIKE THIS BOOK, THEN PLEASE TELL ME! You can email me at **feedback@semsoli.com**, to share with me what you did not like.

Perhaps I can change it.

A book does not have to be stagnant, in today's world. With feedback from readers like yourself, I can improve the book. So, you can impact the quality of this book, and I welcome your feedback. Help make this book better for everyone!

Thank you again for reading this book: I hope you had a good laugh!

OTHER JOKE BOOKS BY JOHNNY RIDDLE

www.ingramcontent.com/pod-product-compliance
Lightning Source LLC
Chambersburg PA
CBHW072023110526
44592CB00012B/1405